OUR SOLAR SYSTEM

Mars

BY DANA MEACHEN RAU

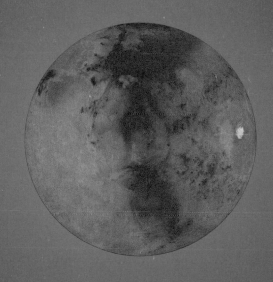

Content Adviser: Dr. Stanley P. Jones, Assistant Director, Washington, D.C., Operations, NASA Classroom of the Future

Science Adviser: Terrence E. Young Jr., M.Ed., M.L.S., Jefferson Parish (La.) Public Schools

Reading Adviser: Dr. Linda D. Labbo, Department of Reading Education, College of Education, The University of Georgia

COMPASS POINT BOOKS

MINNEAPOLIS, MINNESOTA

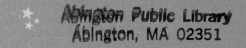
For Chris

Compass Point Books
3722 West 50th Street, #115
Minneapolis, MN 55410

Visit Compass Point Books on the Internet at *www.compasspointbooks.com*
or e-mail your request to *custserv@compasspointbooks.com*

Photographs ©: USGS, cover, 1, 9, 12–13, 14 (all), 15, 16–17; Stock Montage, 4; North Wind Picture Archives, 5, 8; Victoria & Albert Museum, London/Art Resource, NY, 7; NASA, 11, 12 (insert); 17 (insert), 18–19, 20, 21, 22–23; DigitalVision, 24–25; Marilyn Moseley LaMantia/Graphicstock, 26–27.

Editors: E. Russell Primm, Emily J. Dolbear, and Karen Commons
Photo Researchers: Svetlana Zhurkina and Jo Miller
Photo Selector: Karen Commons
Designer: The Design Lab
Illustrator: Graphicstock

Library of Congress Cataloging-in-Publication Data

Rau, Dana Meachen.
    Mars / by Dana Meachen Rau.
        p. cm. — (Our solar system)
    Includes bibliographical references and index.
    Summary: Presents information learned by past and present observers of Mars, the fourth
planet from the sun, and briefly describes the scientific missions that have been sent there.
    ISBN 0-7565-0199-7 (hardcover)
    1. Mars (Planet)—Juvenile literature. [1. Mars (Planet)] I. Title. II. Series: Rau, Dana Meachen.
Our solar system.
  QB641 .R35 2002
  523.43—dc21   2001004416

Table of Contents

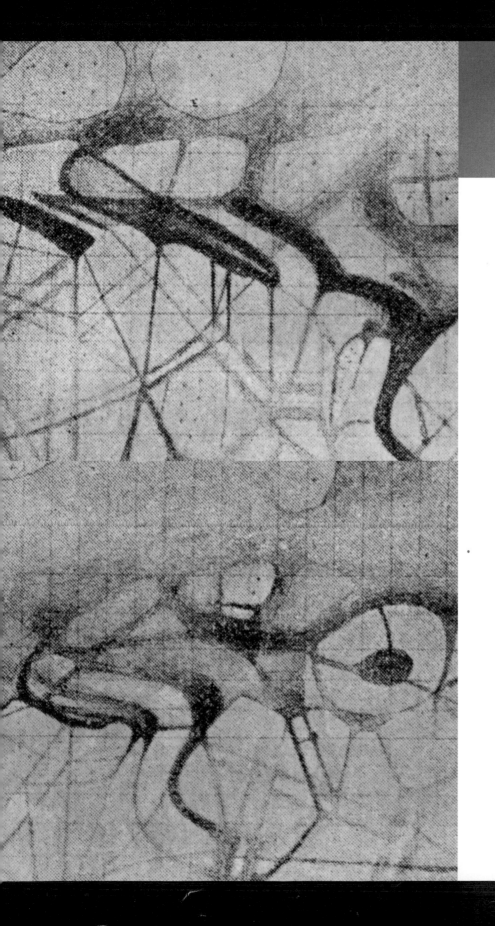

✦ Have you ever read a book about spaceships and aliens from Mars? Many people love reading and writing stories about life on other planets. Creatures from Mars are called Martians. People wonder what Martians might be like.

The idea of life on Mars began in 1877. An Italian **astronomer** named Giovanni Schiaparelli looked through his **telescope** at Mars. Then he drew a map of the lines he

◄◄ *Giovanni Schiaparelli (1835–1910) studied Mars during the late 1800s.*

◄ *Schiaparelli drew this map to show the lines he saw on Mars.*

saw on the surface of Mars. He called these lines "canali." *Canali* is the Italian word for a natural path carved by water. But some people thought Schiaparelli meant he saw "canals." Canals are human-made waterways. So people thought that if Mars had canals, it must have living beings, too.

Today, scientists know this is not true. The natural paths Schiaparelli saw may have been carved by water long ago.

Scientists believe that Mars might once have been a lot like Earth. It may have even had life in the past.

Mars is named after the Roman god of war. The Romans probably gave it this name because it looks red. Red is a color often seen during war. Many people call Mars the "Red Planet." On a clear evening, you can see Mars in the night sky. Its red color can also be seen easily.

Mars, the Roman god of war ▸▸

Looking at the Way Mars Moves

✬ Mars spins, or rotates, in space. The time it takes to rotate is the length of one day on Mars. One day on Mars is about equal to one day on Earth.

Mars orbits, or travels around, the Sun. In 1609, the astronomer Johannes Kepler (1571–1630) looked at Mars in the sky. He thought Mars moved across the sky in a strange way. Up to this time,

Johannes Kepler proved that all planets, ▸ *including Mars, have oval-shaped orbits.*

One of the Viking *spacecraft took* ▸▸ *this picture of Mars's northern ice cap.*

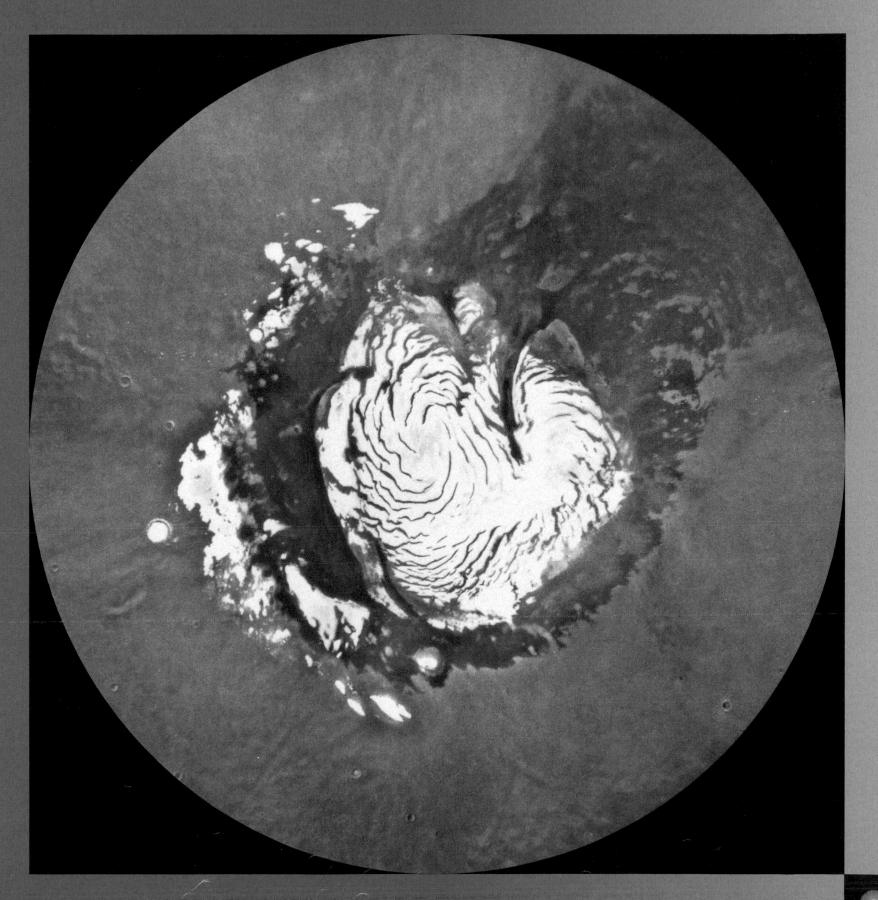

people thought the planets made circle-shaped orbits around the Sun. But the way Mars moved helped prove that planets move in elliptical, or oval-shaped, orbits. Actually, the orbit of Mars is more elliptical than many of the other planets. It takes Mars about two Earth-years to orbit, or revolve around the Sun.

Much like Earth, Mars has **ice caps** at the top and bottom of the planet. The top and bottom are called the north and south **poles**. Also like Earth, each pole on Mars tilts toward the Sun during part of its orbit and tilts away from the Sun at other times. This tilting creates seasons. The ice caps melt during the warmer seasons and grow larger during colder times of the year. But the ice caps on Mars are not made of water like ice on Earth. The ice on Mars is made up of solid carbon dioxide, or "dry ice."

Looking Through Mars

✦ Mercury, Venus, Earth, and Mars are called the rocky planets because they are made mostly of rock. Imagine what Mars would look like if you could cut it in half. Its center is a round, solid **core** made of a metal called iron. Next comes the **mantle**. The mantle is a layer of liquid rock around

◀ *The white spiral with the black dot in the middle is a 1,000-mile (1,600-kilometer)-wide storm. The Hubble Space Telescope took this picture using a special camera that makes Mars look blue.*

the core. Finally, a crust of solid rock covers the mantle.

A planet's atmosphere is made up of the gases around it. Mars has a thin atmosphere of carbon dioxide and other gases. The atmosphere creates weather, such as strong winds and dust storms. Sometimes the strong winds whip the dust and sand around Mars so strongly that astronomers cannot even see the surface of Mars.

The orange cloud at the edge of ▲
Mars's northern ice cap is a 600-mile
(1,000-kilometer)-long dust storm.

A cross-section illustration of Mars ▶
shows its core, mantle, and crust.

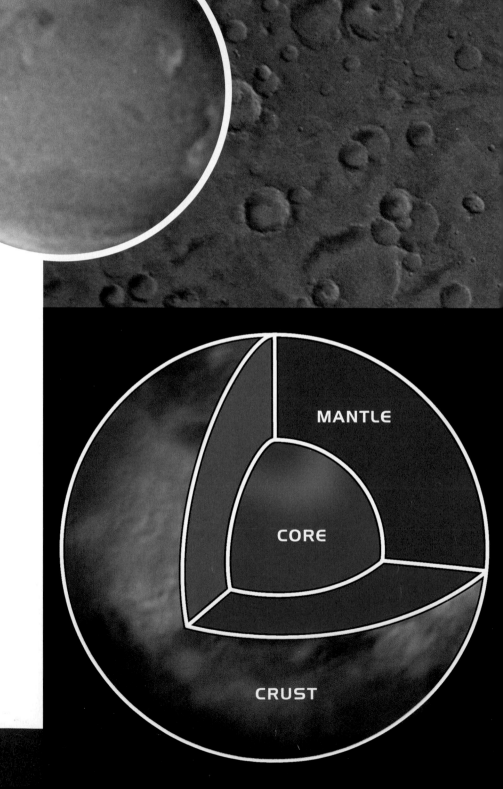

MANTLE

CORE

CRUST

Looking at the Surface of Mars

✦ The surface of Mars has many kinds of landforms. The northern hemisphere (the top half of Mars) has many flat areas called plains. The southern hemisphere (the bottom half) has deep holes called craters. **Volcanoes** cover much of the surface of Mars. Long ago, they shot out **lava** that created many of the landforms we see on Mars today. Olympus Mons is the largest volcano on Mars at 17 miles (27 kilometers) high. It is also the largest

◂ *This region in the southern hemisphere of Mars is full of craters.*

mountain in the **solar system.**

Some scientists believe that rivers of water may have carved deep **can-yons** on Mars a long time ago. A series of can-yons called Valles Marineris is up to 6 miles (10 kilome-ters) deep in some places. It is also more than 2,486 miles (4,000 kilometers) long. The Valles Marineris canyon sys-tem is so big that it would reach across the entire United States!

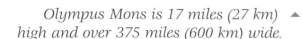

Olympus Mons is 17 miles (27 km) ▲
high and over 375 miles (600 km) wide.

This region in the northern hemisphere ▶
of Mars is very smooth.

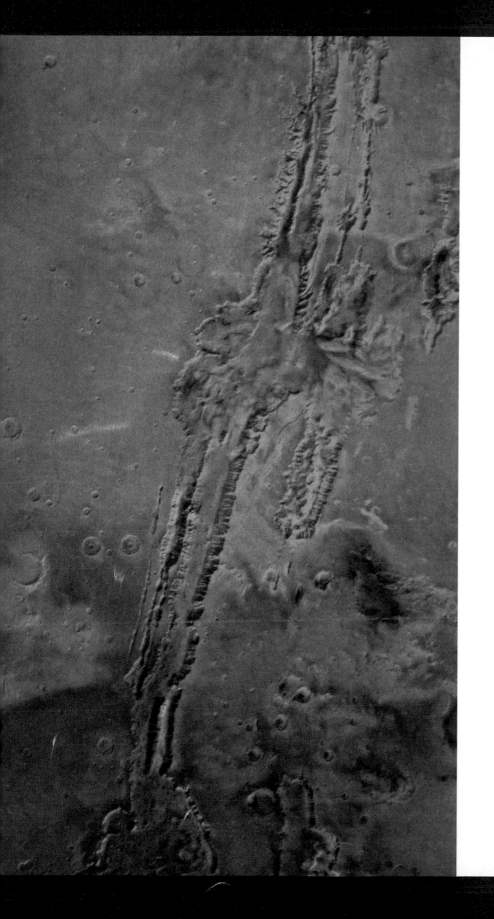

Scientists have not found water on Mars. But some believe that Mars may have water under the ground. Water may be only 300 to 1,300 feet (90 to 400 meters) below the surface.

The **temperature** of Mars changes from season to season. During the summer, the temperature on Mars can reach 70° Fahrenheit (20° Celsius), like many places on Earth. But during the winter on Mars, the temperature can be as low as –230° F (–140° C)! Usually, the temperature on the surface of Mars is far below freezing.

◄ *The Valles Marineris canyon system might have been formed long ago by rivers of water.*

Looking Around Mars

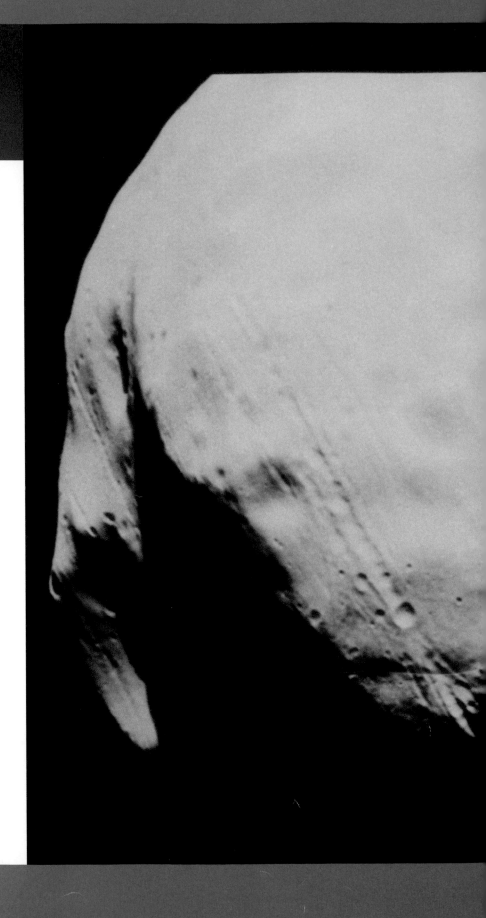

Two moons orbit Mars. They were discovered by Asaph Hall (1829–1907), an American astronomer, in 1877. Scientists named them *Phobos* and *Deimos*. These are Greek names meaning Fear and Terror. Both Phobos and Deimos are tiny. In fact, Deimos is the smallest moon in the solar system. Phobos moves very quickly around Mars—it takes about seven and one half hours to complete one orbit. At certain points on

The moon Phobos has huge craters ▶
and a lumpy surface.

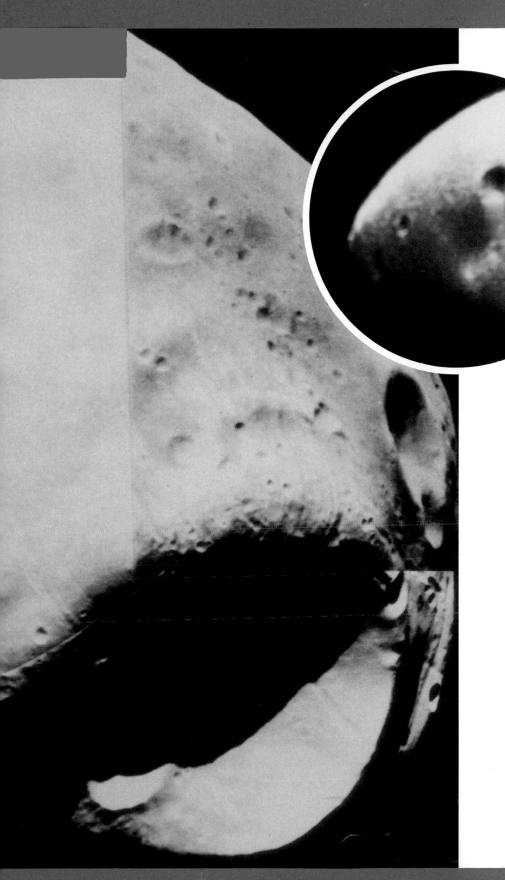

Mars, Phobos rises and sets in the sky twice a day! The surfaces of both moons are covered with craters and grooves.

Some scientists believe Phobos and Deimos may have once been asteroids. Asteroids are pieces of rock that revolve around the Sun between the orbits of Mars and Jupiter. They believe that Mars "captured" Phobos and Deimos into orbit because they are not round like most

▲ *Deimos is a tiny moon with an unusual shape.* Viking 1 *took this picture using a special camera that makes the edges of some of the craters look orange.*

planets and moons. Instead, they are irregular chunks of rock and ice.

Many scientists believe that Mars will not always have moons. In about 50 million years, both moons may be lost. Phobos orbits so near to Mars that the planet is slowly pulling it in. Someday, the moon will either crash into the planet or break into lots of smaller pieces. Deimos is actually moving away from Mars. Someday it will get so far away that the pull of Mars won't be strong enough to keep it in orbit.

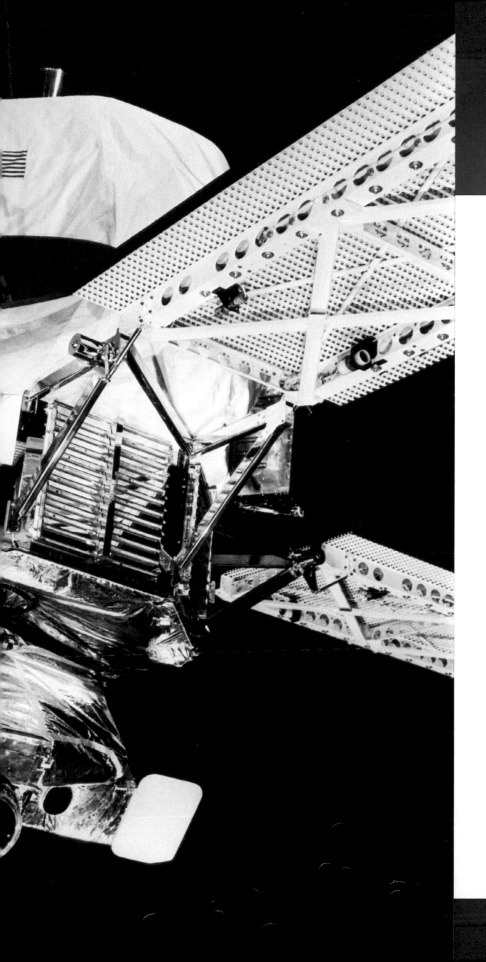

Looking at Mars from Space

★ Spacecraft are an important tool for scientists. Sometimes they send spacecraft on missions to study the planets. Mars has been visited by more spacecraft than any other planet. More than thirty missions have been sent to the Red Planet.

Mariner 4 flew by Mars in 1965, and *Mariners 6* and *7* flew by in 1969. Then, in 1971, *Mariner 9* became the first spacecraft to orbit another planet. These spacecraft sent

◀ Mariner 9 *was the first spacecraft to orbit another planet.*

back pictures and information about Mars to Earth.

In 1976, two *Viking* spacecraft landed on Mars. Both *Viking* spacecraft were looking for life on Mars. Each spacecraft had two parts. One part orbited the planet while the other part landed on the surface. The **landers** sent back information about the soil, wind, and temperature of the planet. From this information, astronomers decided there was probably no life on Mars.

Mars Pathfinder landed on the surface of Mars on July 4, 1997. It brought along a small

The Viking 2 *lander studied the* ▶ *surface of Mars.*

car, or rover, named Sojourner. Sojourner rolled around on the ground. It was a very exciting mission. *Mars Pathfinder* studied the atmosphere of Mars, took pictures of the

▲ Mars Pathfinder's *rover,* Sojourner, *drove down a ramp and across the Martian surface to study Mars's rocks and soil.*

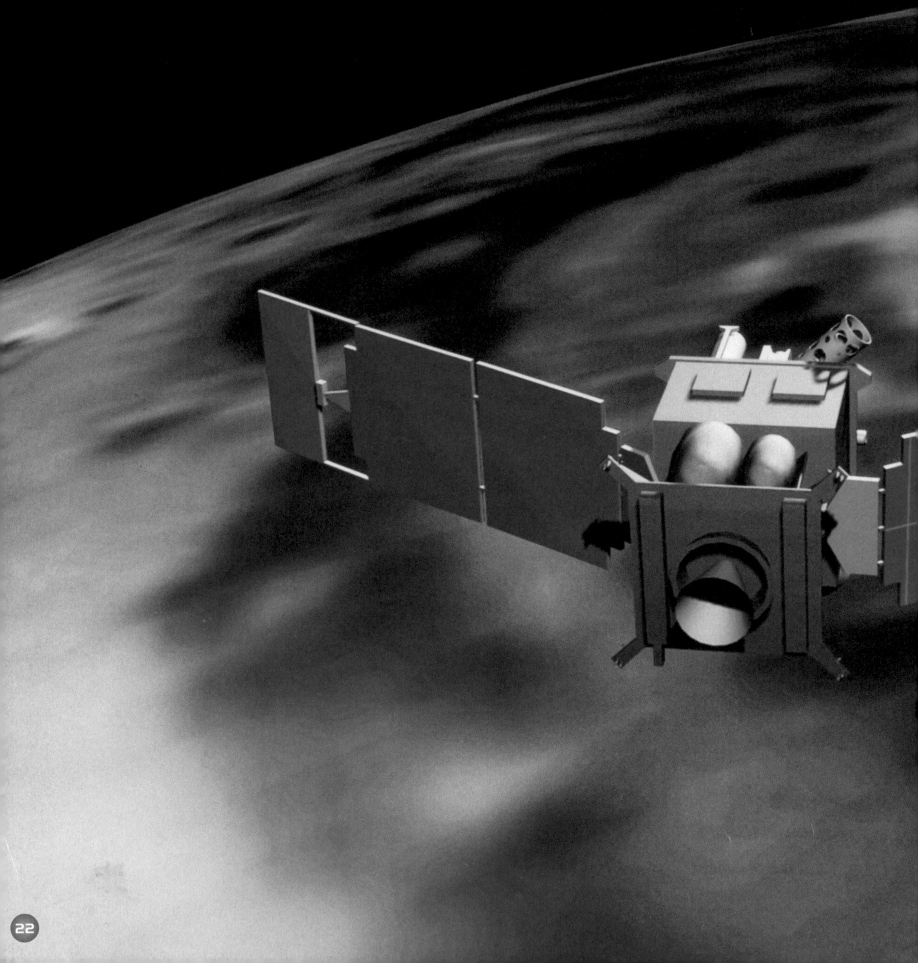

planet's surface, and examined the rocks and soil at the landing site. It sent back a lot of information.

The *Mars Global Surveyor* reached Mars in September 1997. It orbited Mars and made a map of the surface. It also found clues that showed there might be liquid water under the ground. Once again, astronomers began to wonder about life on Mars today or in the past.

◀ *The* Mars Global Surveyor *reached Mars on September 11, 1997.*

Looking to the Future

⋆ After the *Mars Global Surveyor,* even more space-craft were sent to Mars. And more missions are planned. But not all missions are successful. Both the *Mars Climate Orbiter* in 1998 and the *Mars Polar Lander* in 1999 were lost as they neared Mars.

Scientists are considering sending people to Mars in the future. If people do land on Mars, they will have traveled farther into space than anyone before them. People might be able to live on Mars

if there is water under the surface. However, scientists need to learn more about how space affects people's bodies before sending them to the Red Planet.

◀ *This is how scientists imagine a human visit to Mars might look.*

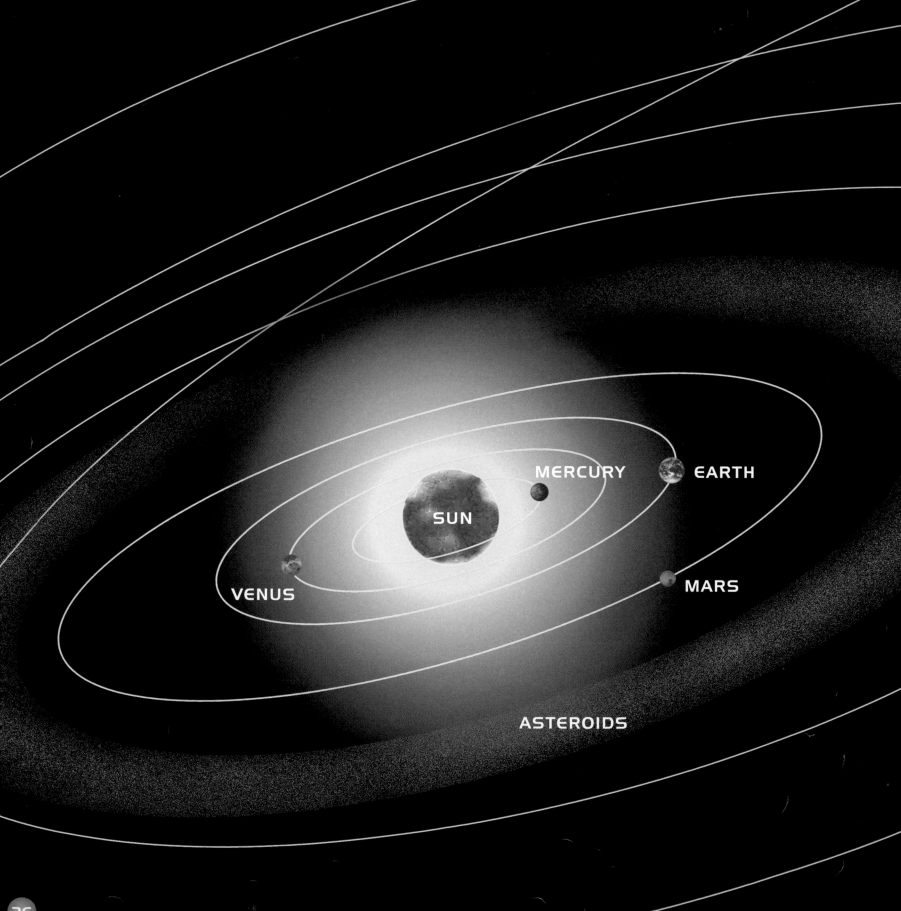

JUPITER

URANUS

SATURN

NEPTUNE

PLUTO

Glossary

astronomer—someone who studies space

canyons—deep valleys with steep sides

core—the center of a planet

ice caps—covers of ice and snow

landers—parts of spacecraft that land on a planet's surface

lava—liquid rock

mantle—a layer inside a planet often made of hot liquid

poles—the northernmost and southernmost points on a planet

solar system—a group of objects in space including the Sun, planets, moons, asteroids, comets, and meteoroids

telescope—a tool astronomers use to make objects look closer

temperature—how hot or cold something is

volcanos—mountains that may erupt with hot liquid rock

A Mars Flyby

Mars is the third smallest planet, after Pluto and Mercury, and the fourth planet from the Sun.

If you weighed 75 pounds (34 kilograms) on Earth, you would weigh 29 pounds (13 kilograms) on Mars.

Average distance from the Sun: 142 million miles (228 million kilometers)

Distance from Earth: 34 million miles (54.5 million kilometers) to 249 million miles (401 million kilometers)

Diameter: 4,222 miles (6,794 kilometers)

Number of times Mars would fit inside Earth: 7

Did You Know?

- Mars looks red in space because its soil is covered by rust.

- The month of March was also named after Mars, the Roman god of war.

- A very large crater named Stickney covers a large part of the surface of Phobos, one of the two moons of Mars.

- *Viking 1* took a picture of a landform on Mars's surface that looks like a giant face. It probably looks this way because the light was hitting the mountains and cliffs.

- More than thirty missions have been sent to Mars. That is more than any other planet.

- Some important missions that went to Mars are: *Mariner 4, Mariner 6, Mariner 7, Mariner 9, Viking 1, Viking 2, Mars Pathfinder,* and *Mars Global Surveyor.*

- When *Mariner 9* arrived at Mars in 1971, it had trouble seeing the surface because of a giant dust storm that lasted for months!

- When the *Mars Pathfinder* lander fell to the surface, it bounced along the ground on airbags like a big rubber ball.

- In 1996, scientists found a very tiny organism in a meteorite that they believe came from Mars. It may help prove that there was once life on the planet.

- A trip from Earth to Mars and back might take around 972 days—258 days to get to Mars, 455 days on the surface, and 259 days to get home. That is almost three years!

Time it takes to orbit around Sun (one Mars year): 687 Earth-days

Time it takes to rotate (one Mars day): 24.6 Earth-hours

Structure: core (solid iron)
mantle (liquid rock)
crust (solid rock)

Average surface temperature: -85° Fahrenheit (-65° Celsius)

Atmosphere: carbon dioxide, nitrogen, argon, oxygen, carbon monoxide

Atmospheric pressure (Earth=1.0) : 0.007

Moons: 2

Rings: 0

Want to Know More?

AT THE LIBRARY

Fradin, Dennis B. *Is There Life on Mars?* New York: McElderry Books, 1999.
Redfern, Martin. *The Kingfisher Young People's Book of Space.* New York: Kingfisher, 1998.
Spangenburg, Ray and Kit Moser. *A Look at Mars.* Danbury, Conn.: Franklin Watts, 2000.
Vogt, Gregory. *Mars.* Austin, Tex.: Steadwell Books, 2001.

ON THE WEB

Exploring the Planets: Mars
http://www.nasm.edu/ceps/etp/mars/
MARS.html
For more information about Mars

NASA Observatorium: Mars
http://observe.ivv.nasa.gov/nasa/exhibits/
mars/mars_home.html
For information, pictures, stories, and
games about Mars

The Nine Planets: Mars
http://www.seds.org/nineplanets/nineplan-
ets/mars.html
For a multimedia tour of Mars and its
moons

Solar System Exploration:
Missions to Mars
*http://sse.jpl.nasa.gov/missions/mars_*
missns/mars-mgs.html
For more information about important
NASA missions to the Red Planet

Space Kids
http://spacekids.hq.nasa.gov/2003/
For information about the next mission
to Mars and how to send your name up
with the spacecraft

Space.com
http://www.space.com
For the latest news about everything to do
with space

Star Date Online: Mars
http://www.stardate.org/resources/ssguide/
mars.html
For an overview of Mars and hints on
where it can be seen in the sky

Welcome to the Planets: Mars
http://pds.jpl.nasa.gov/planets/choices/
mars1.htm
For pictures and information about Mars
and some of its most important surface
features

THROUGH THE MAIL

Goddard Space Flight Center
Code 130, Public Affairs Office
Greenbelt, MD 20771
To learn more about space exploration

Jet Propulsion Laboratory
4800 Oak Grove Drive
Pasadena, CA 91109
To learn more about the spacecraft
missions

Lunar and Planetary Institute
3600 Bay Area Boulevard
Houston, TX 77058
To learn more about Mars and
other planets

Space Science Division
NASA Ames Research Center
Moffet Field, CA 94035
To learn more about Mars and
solar system exploration

ON THE ROAD

**Adler Planetarium and
Astronomy Museum**
1300 S. Lake Shore Drive
Chicago, IL 60605-2403
312/922-STAR
To visit the oldest planetarium
in the Western Hemisphere

***Exploring the Planets* and
*Where Next Columbus?***
National Air and Space Museum
7th and Independence Avenue, S.W.
Washington, DC 20560
202/357-2700
To learn more about the solar system
and see models of the *Mars Pathfinder*
lander and *Sojourner* rover

**Rose Center for Earth and
Space/Hayden Planetarium**
Central Park West at 79th Street
New York, NY 10024-5192
212/769-5100
To visit this new planetarium and
learn more about the planets

UCO/Lick Observatory
University of California
Santa Cruz, CA 95064
408/274-5061
To see the telescope that was used to
discover the first planets outside of
our solar system

Index

◄ **About the Author:** *Dana Meachen Rau loves to study space. Her office walls are covered with pictures of planets, astronauts, and spacecraft. She also likes to look up at the sky with her telescope and write poems about what she sees. Ms. Rau is the author of more than sixty books for children, including nonfiction, biographies, storybooks, and early readers. She lives in Farmington, Connecticut, with her husband, Chris, and children, Charlie and Allison.*